GRAPHIC SCIENCE

DECODING GENES

WITH MAX AXIOM

SUPER SCIENTIST

by Amber J. Keyser, PhD

illustrated by Tod G. Smith and Al Milgrom

Consultant:
Monte Westerfield, PhD
Professor of Biology
University of Oregon

CAPSTONE PRESS
a capstone imprint

Graphic Library is published by Capstone Press,
151 Good Counsel Drive, P.O. Box 669, Mankato, Minnesota 56002.
www.capstonepress.com

Printed in the United States of America in Stevens Point, Wisconsin.

092009
005619WZS10

Books published by Capstone Press are manufactured with paper containing at least 10 percent post-consumer waste.

Library of Congress Cataloging-in-Publication Data
Keyser, Amber.
Decoding genes with Max Axiom, super scientist / by Amber J. Keyser ; illustrated by Tod G. Smith and Al Milgrom.
p. cm.—(Graphic library. Graphic science.)
Summary: "In graphic novel format, follows the adventures of Max Axiom as he explains the science behind genes" — Provided by publisher.
Includes bibliographical references and index.
ISBN 978-1-4296-3976-7 (library binding)
ISBN 978-1-4296-4862-2 (paperback)
1. Genes — Comic books, strips, etc. — Juvenile literature. 2. DNA — Comic books, strips, etc. — Juvenile literature. I. Smith, Tod, ill. II. Milgrom, A. (Allen), ill. III. Title.
QH447.K47 2010
576.5 — dc22 2009039894

Designer
Alison Thiele

Cover Colorist
Krista Ward

Colorist
Matt Webb

Media Researcher
Wanda Winch

Production Specialist
Laura Manthe

Editor
Mari Bolte

TABLE OF CONTENTS

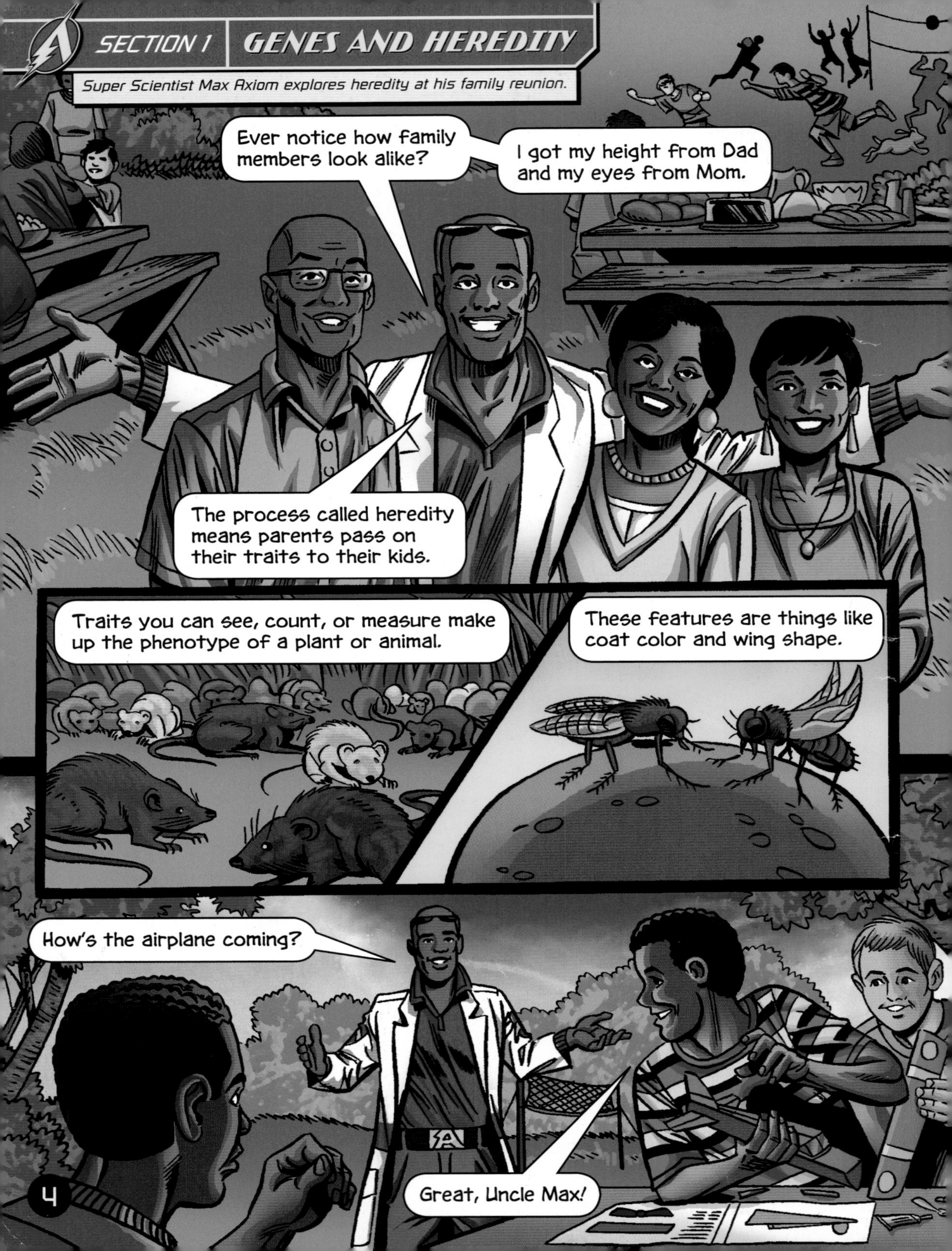
SECTION 1
GENES AND HEREDITY
Super Scientist Max Axiom explores heredity at his family reunion.
Ever notice how family members look alike?
I got my height from Dad and my eyes from Mom.
The process called heredity means parents pass on their traits to their kids.
Traits you can see, count, or measure make up the phenotype of a plant or animal.
These features are things like coat color and wing shape.
How's the airplane coming?
Great, Uncle Max!

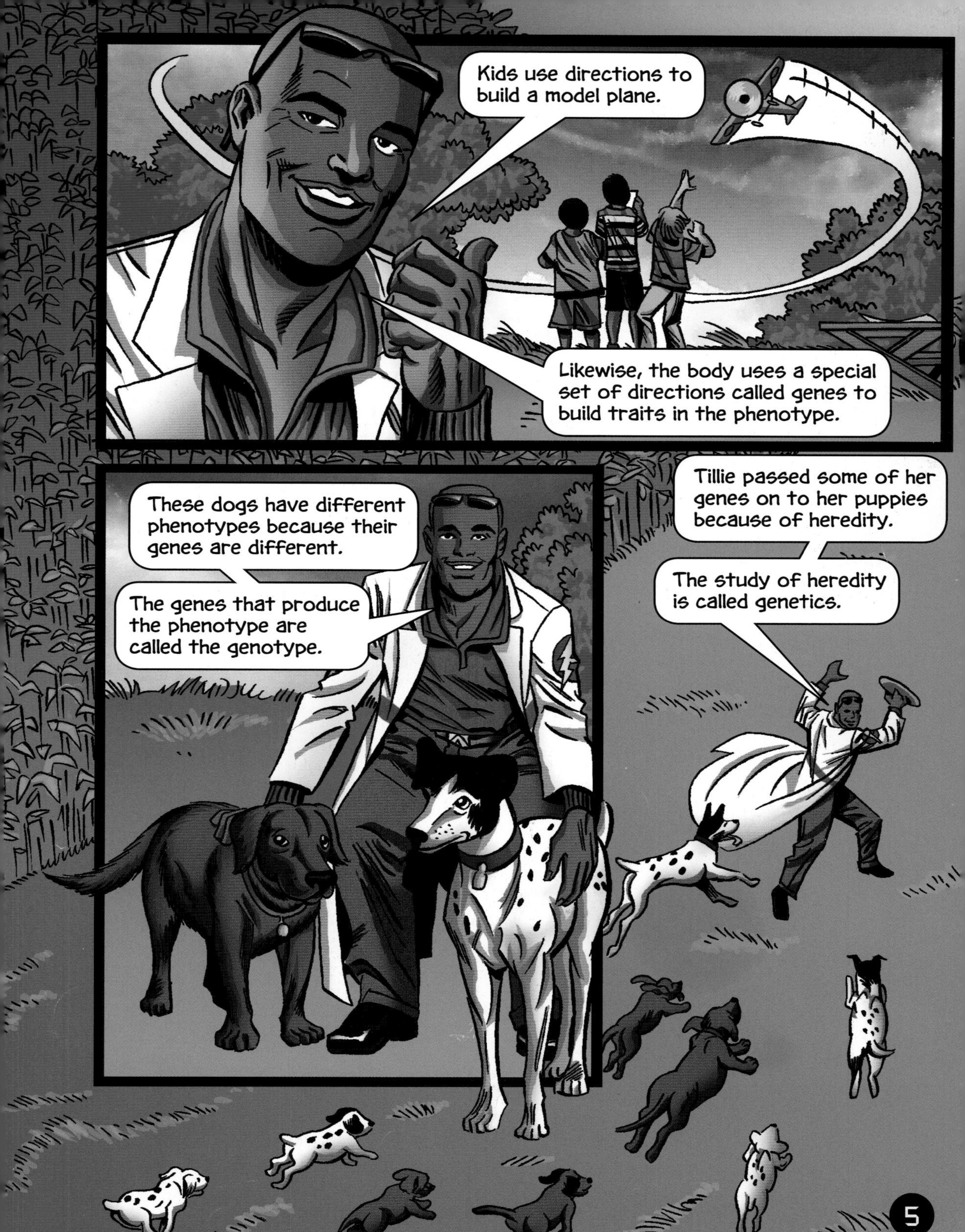
Kids use directions to build a model plane.
Likewise, the body uses a special set of directions called genes to build traits in the phenotype.
These dogs have different phenotypes because their genes are different.
The genes that produce the phenotype are called the genotype.
Tillie passed some of her genes on to her puppies because of heredity.
The study of heredity is called genetics.

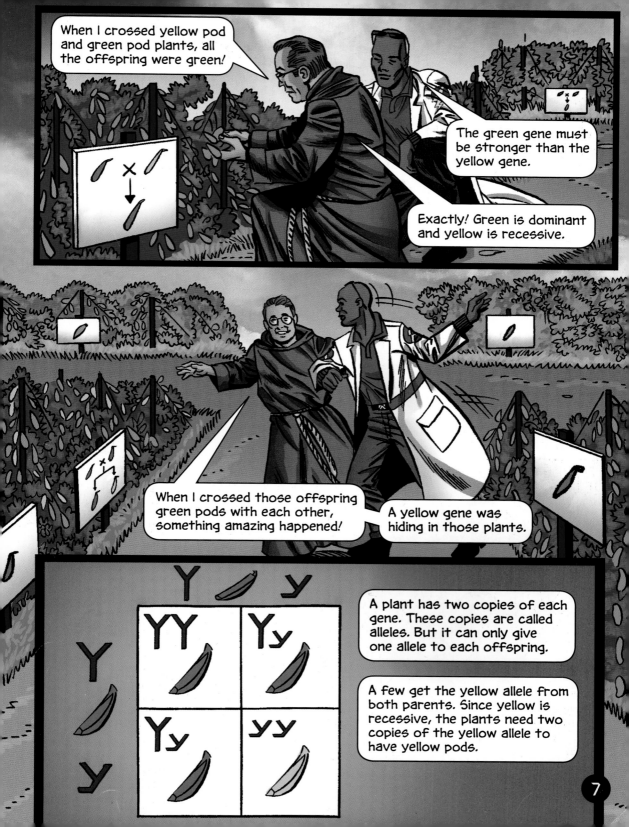

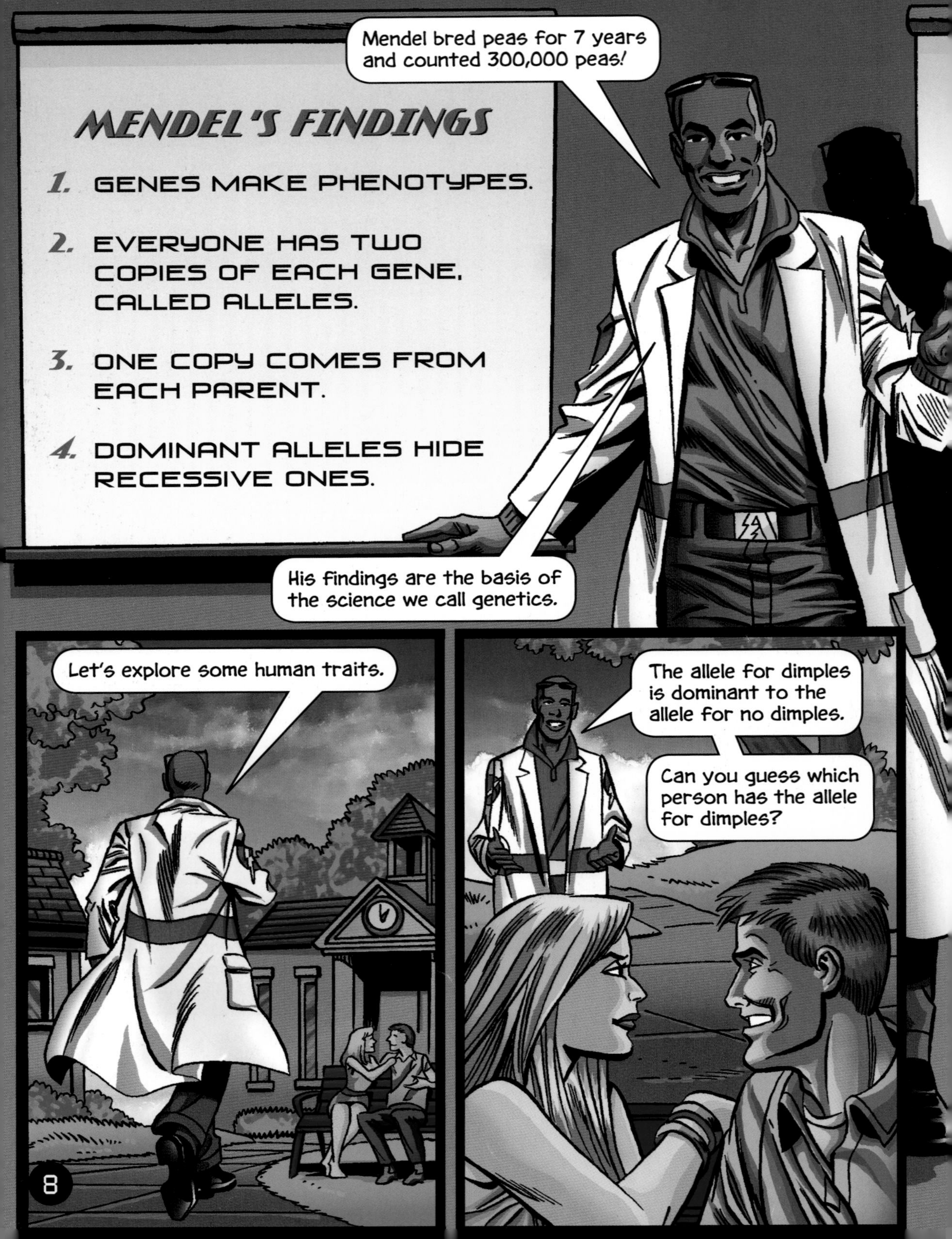
Mendel bred peas for 7 years and counted 300,000 peas!
MENDEL'S FINDINGS
1. GENES MAKE PHENOTYPES.
2. EVERYONE HAS TWO COPIES OF EACH GENE, CALLED ALLELES.
3. ONE COPY COMES FROM EACH PARENT.
4. DOMINANT ALLELES HIDE RECESSIVE ONES.
His findings are the basis of the science we call genetics.
Let's explore some human traits.
The allele for dimples is dominant to the allele for no dimples.
Can you guess which person has the allele for dimples?

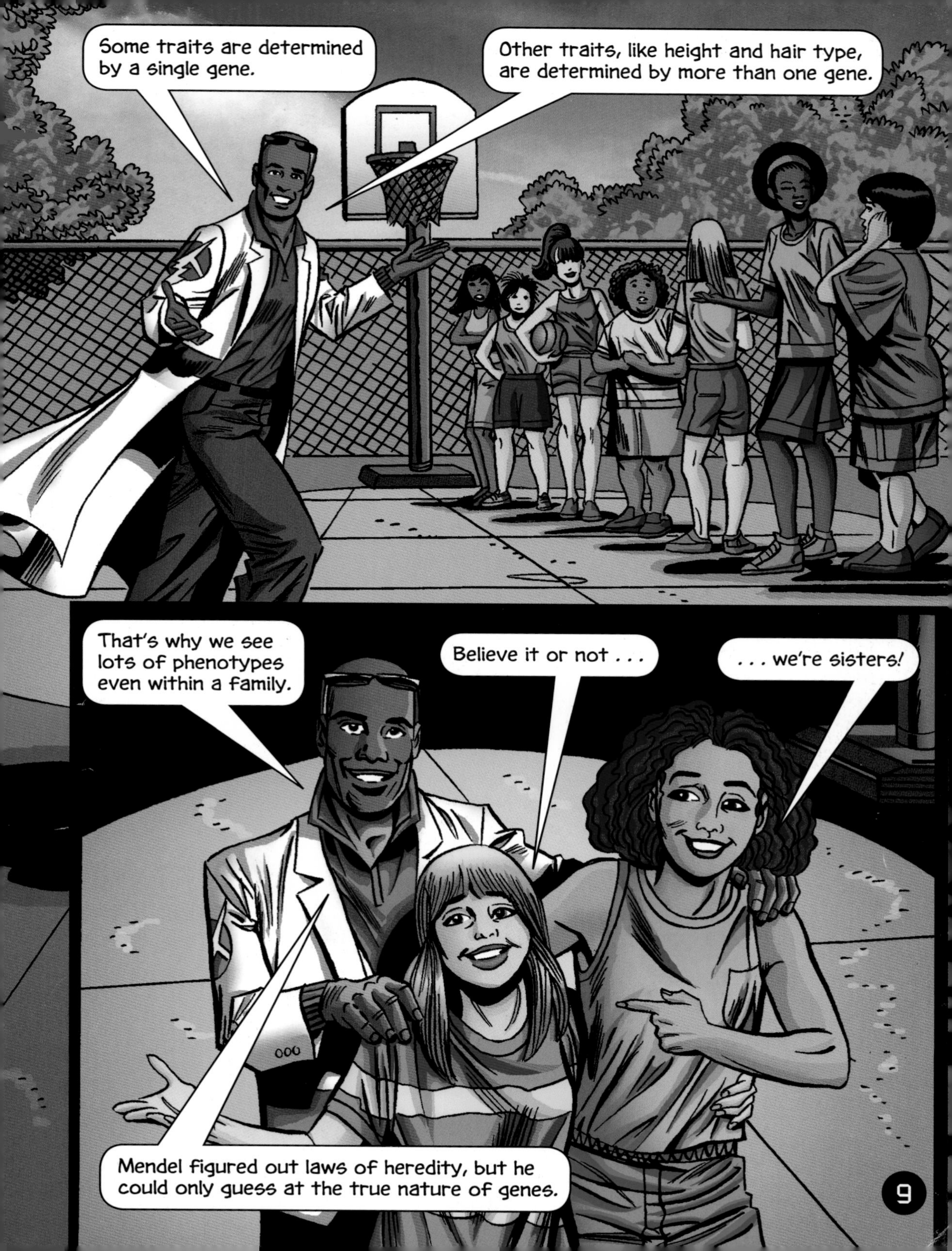
Some traits are determined by a single gene.
Other traits, like height and hair type, are determined by more than one gene.
That's why we see lots of phenotypes even within a family.
Believe it or not . . .
. . . we're sisters!
Mendel figured out laws of heredity, but he could only guess at the true nature of genes.

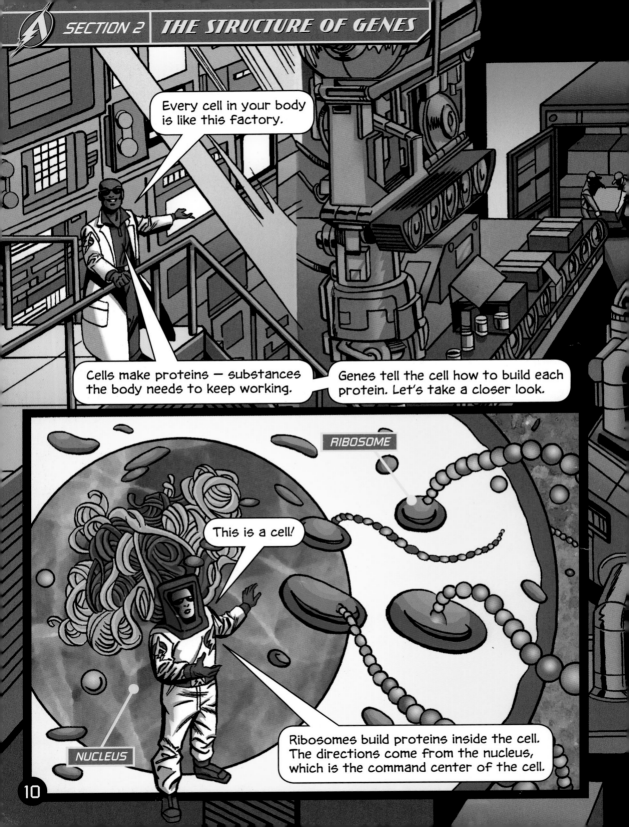

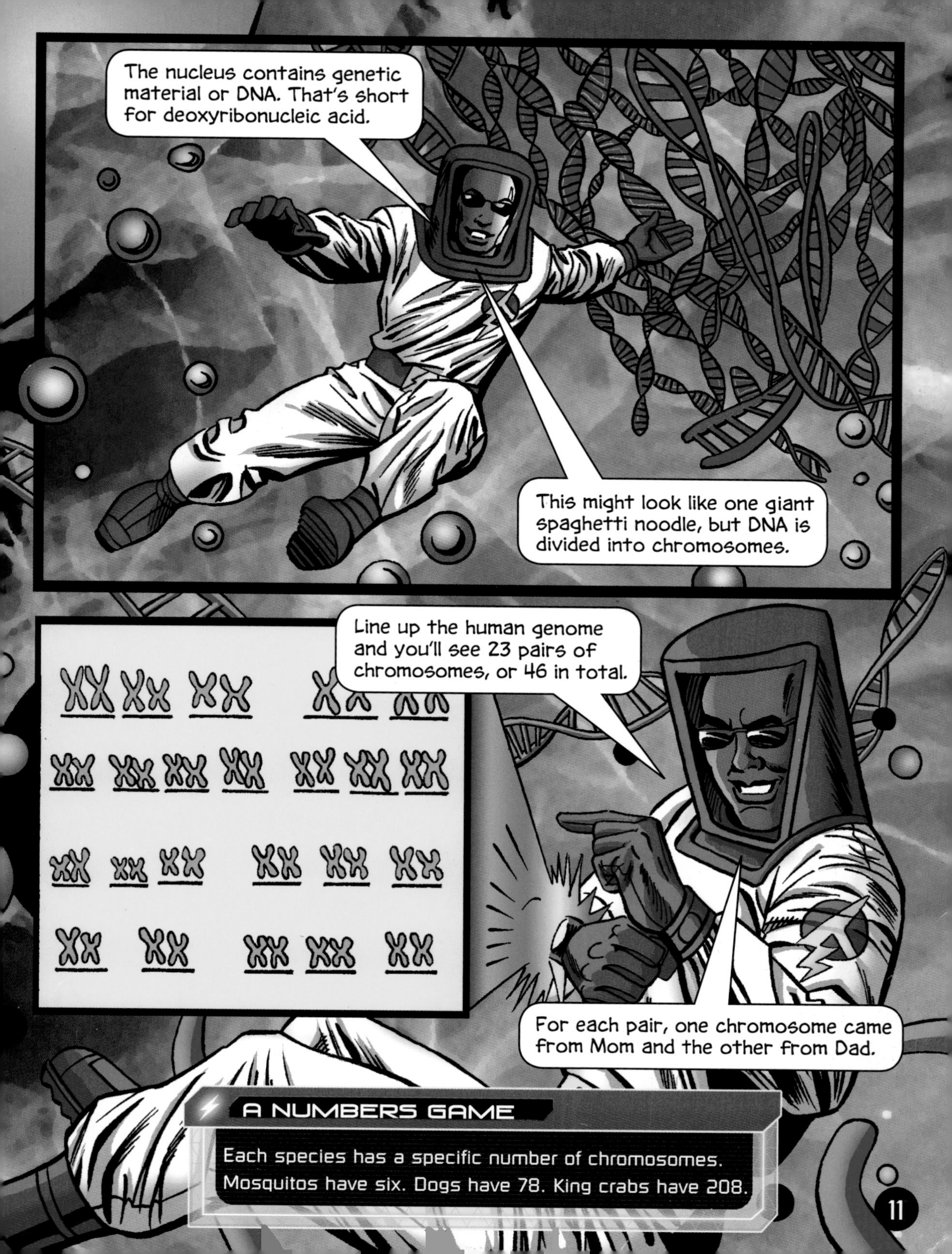

The nucleus contains genetic material or DNA. That's short for deoxyribonucleic acid.
This might look like one giant spaghetti noodle, but DNA is divided into chromosomes.
Line up the human genome and you'll see 23 pairs of chromosomes, or 46 in total.
For each pair, one chromosome came from Mom and the other from Dad.
A NUMBERS GAME
Each species has a specific number of chromosomes. Mosquitos have six. Dogs have 78. King crabs have 208.

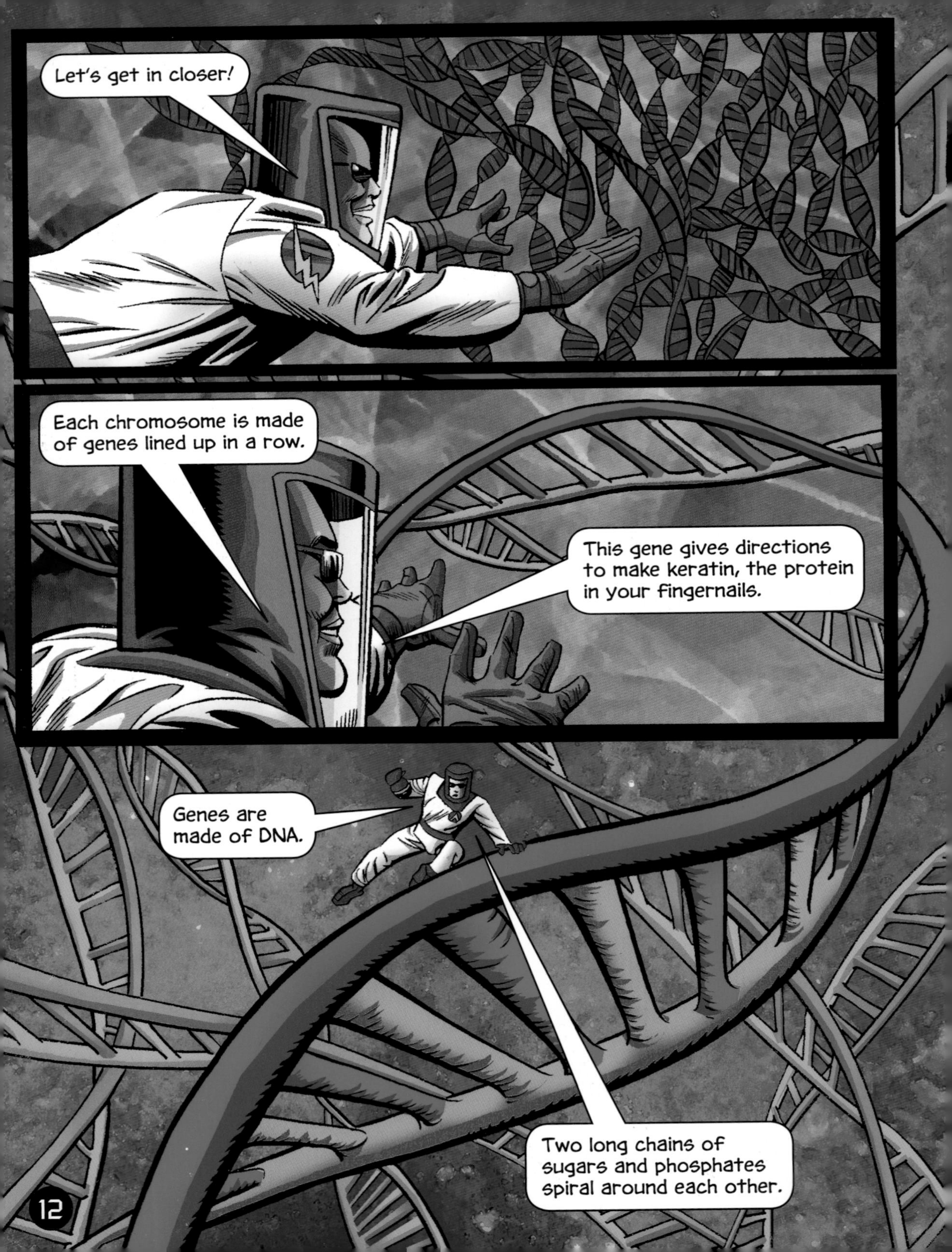
Let's get in closer!
Each chromosome is made of genes lined up in a row.
This gene gives directions to make keratin, the protein in your fingernails.
Genes are made of DNA.
Two long chains of sugars and phosphates spiral around each other.

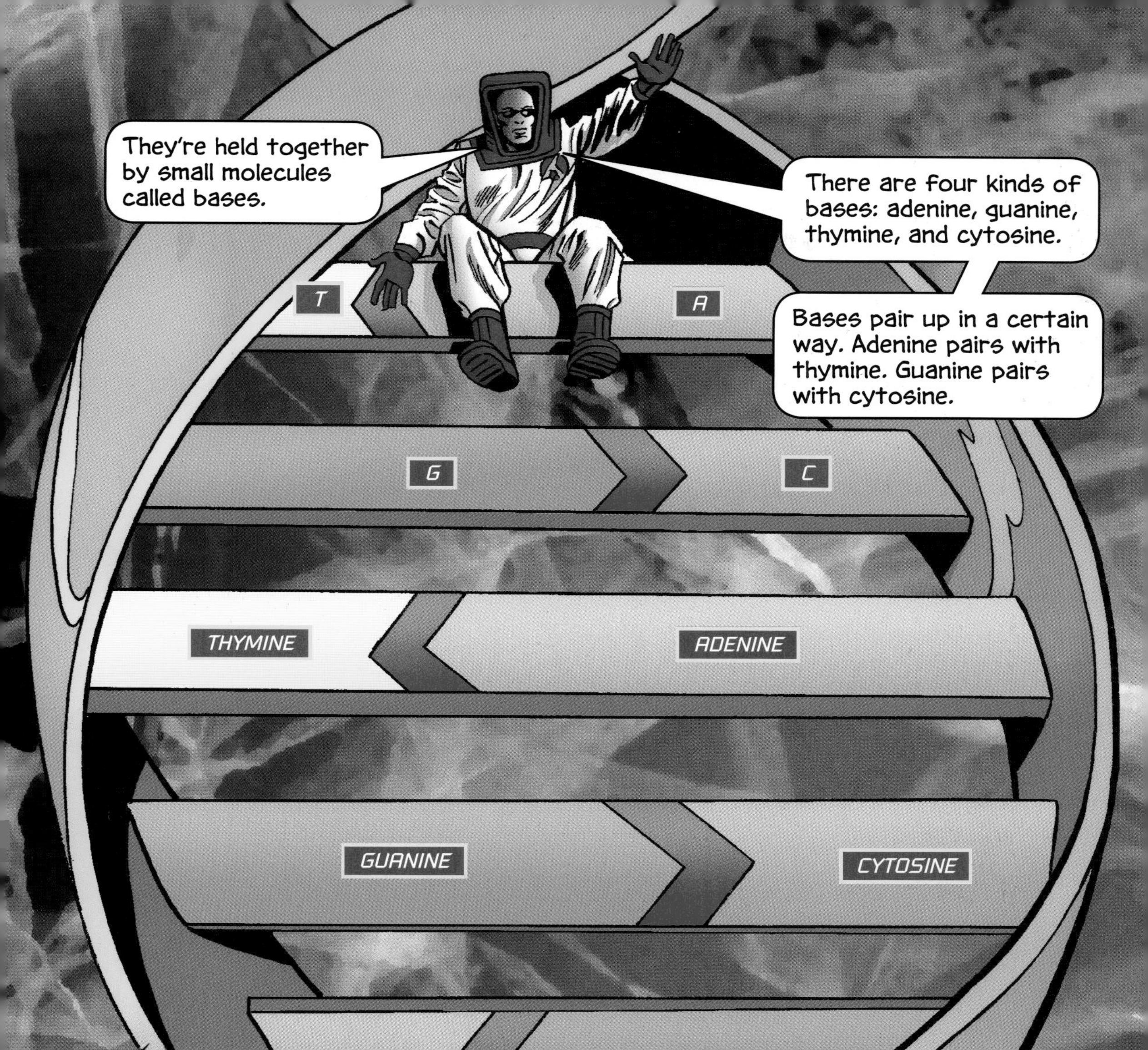
They're held together by small molecules called bases.
There are four kinds of bases: adenine, guanine, thymine, and cytosine.
Bases pair up in a certain way. Adenine pairs with thymine. Guanine pairs with cytosine.
T
A
G
C
THYMINE
ADENINE
GUANINE
CYTOSINE

STRUCTURE OF DNA

ACCESS GRANTED: MAX AXIOM

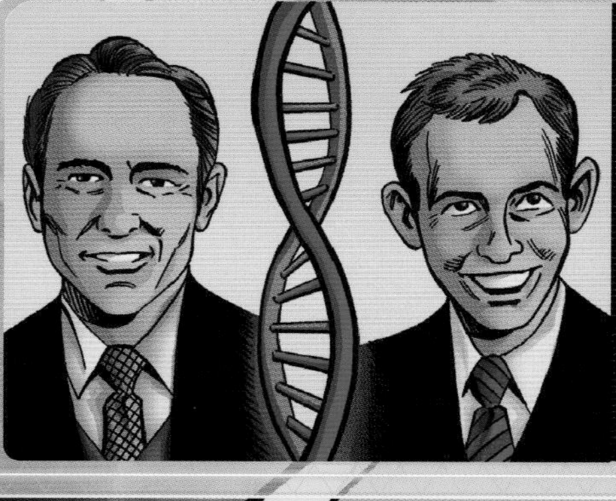

In 1953, Francis Crick and James Watson discovered the structure of DNA. By doing this, they won a great scientific race to unravel the puzzle of heredity. Both later acknowledged that they couldn't have done it without Rosalind Franklin's help. She took a special picture of DNA using X-ray crystallography.

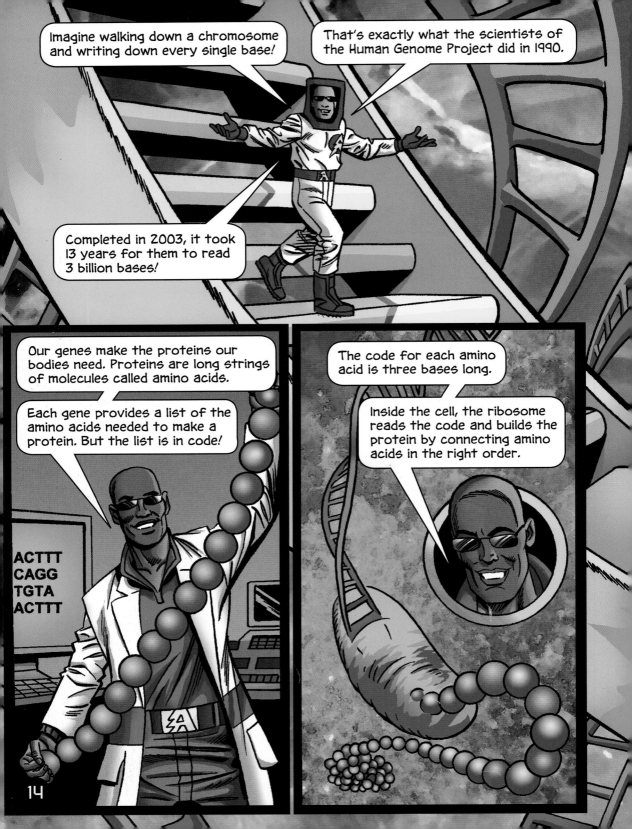

Imagine walking down a chromosome and writing down every single base!

That's exactly what the scientists of the Human Genome Project did in 1990.

Completed in 2003, it took 13 years for them to read 3 billion bases!

Our genes make the proteins our bodies need. Proteins are long strings of molecules called amino acids.

Each gene provides a list of the amino acids needed to make a protein. But the list is in code!

The code for each amino acid is three bases long.

Inside the cell, the ribosome reads the code and builds the protein by connecting amino acids in the right order.

ACTTT
CAGG
TGTA
ACTTT

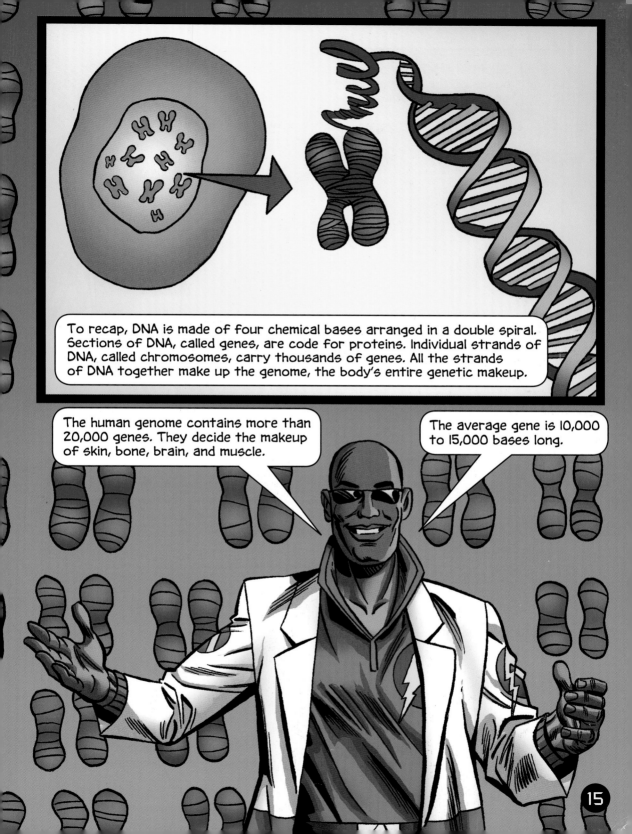

To recap, DNA is made of four chemical bases arranged in a double spiral. Sections of DNA, called genes, are code for proteins. Individual strands of DNA, called chromosomes, carry thousands of genes. All the strands of DNA together make up the genome, the body's entire genetic makeup.

The human genome contains more than 20,000 genes. They decide the makeup of skin, bone, brain, and muscle.

The average gene is 10,000 to 15,000 bases long.

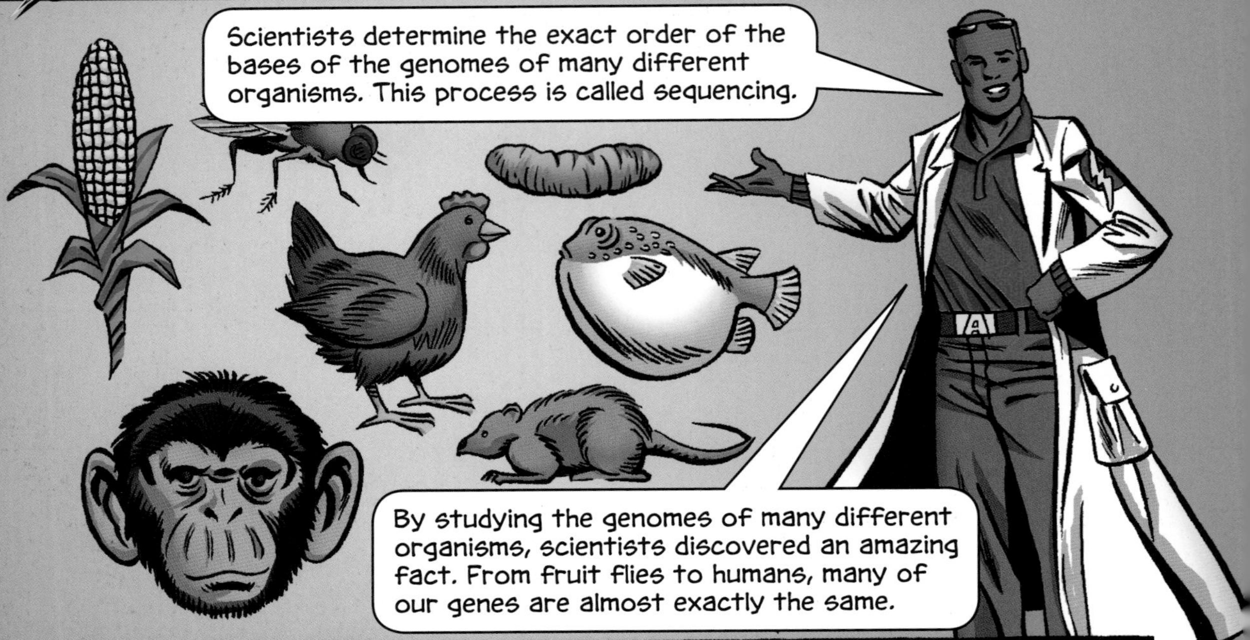
Scientists determine the exact order of the bases of the genomes of many different organisms. This process is called sequencing.
By studying the genomes of many different organisms, scientists discovered an amazing fact. From fruit flies to humans, many of our genes are almost exactly the same.

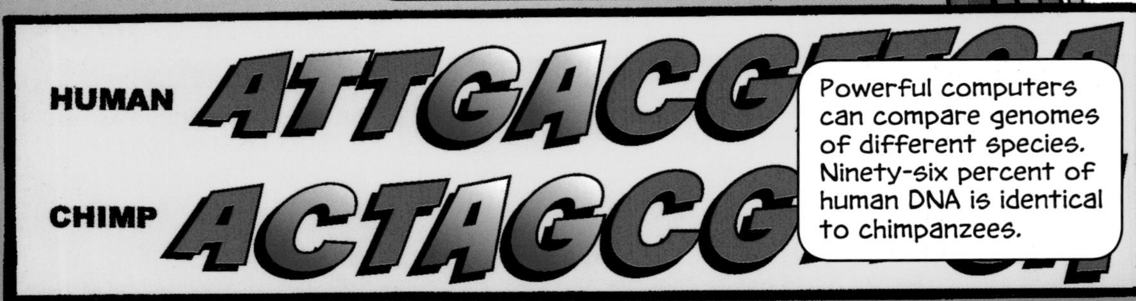
HUMAN ATTGACG
CHIMP ACTAGCG
Powerful computers can compare genomes of different species. Ninety-six percent of human DNA is identical to chimpanzees.

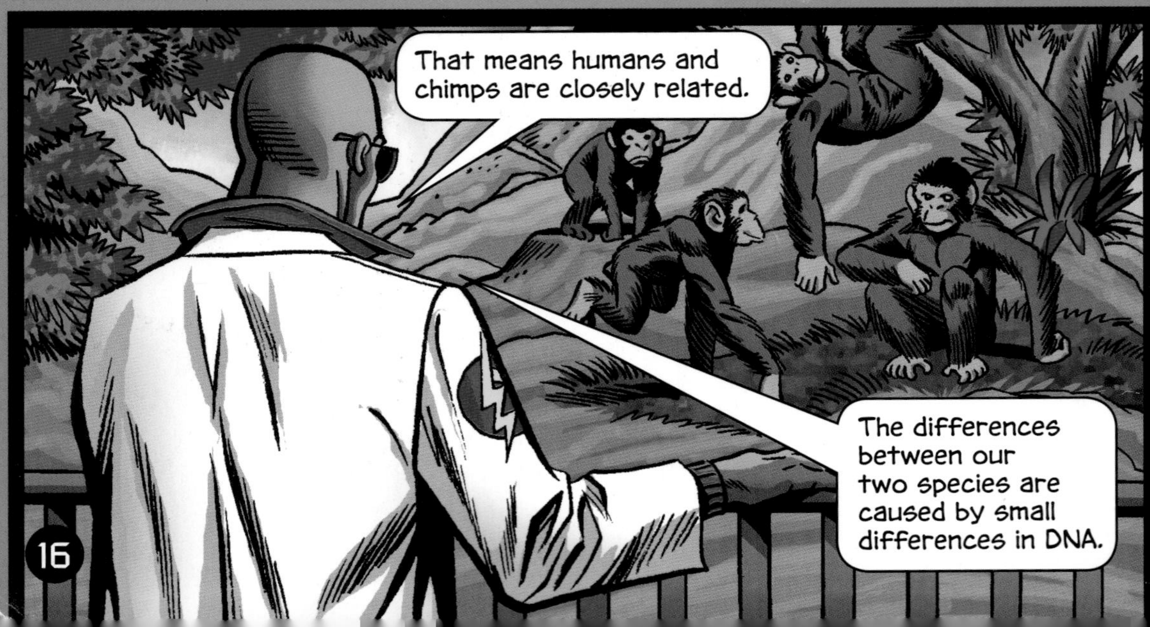
That means humans and chimps are closely related.
The differences between our two species are caused by small differences in DNA.

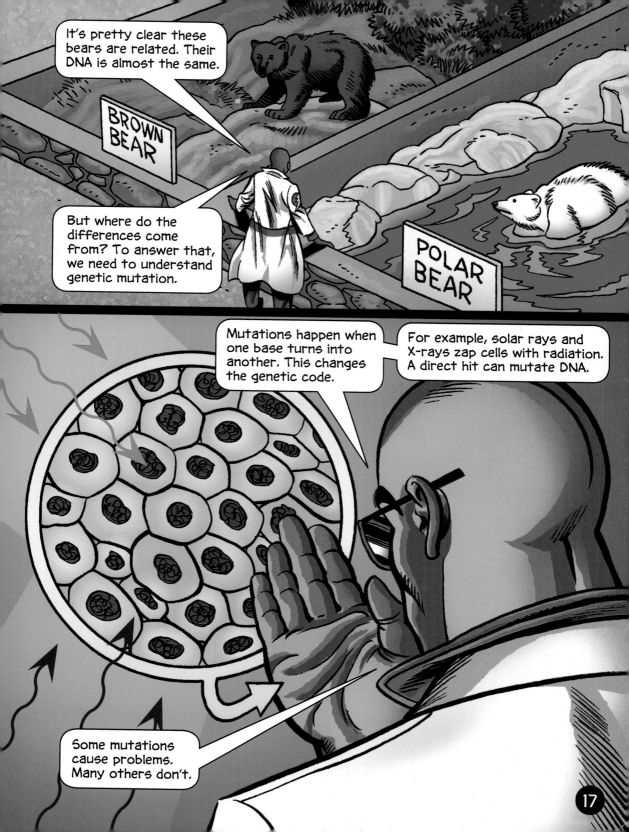

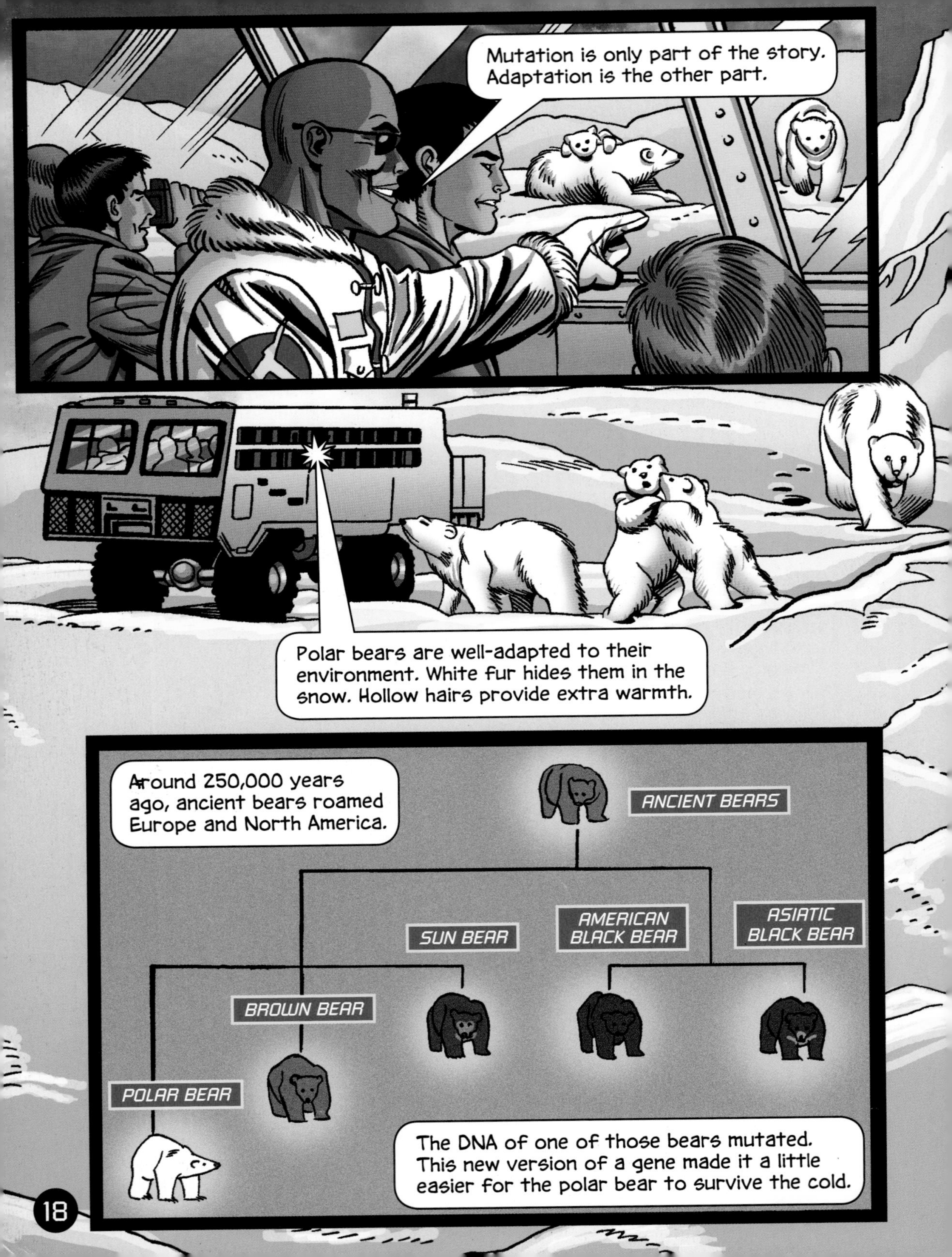

Mutation is only part of the story. Adaptation is the other part.
Polar bears are well-adapted to their environment. White fur hides them in the snow. Hollow hairs provide extra warmth.
Around 250,000 years ago, ancient bears roamed Europe and North America.
ANCIENT BEARS
SUN BEAR
AMERICAN BLACK BEAR
ASIATIC BLACK BEAR
BROWN BEAR
POLAR BEAR
The DNA of one of those bears mutated. This new version of a gene made it a little easier for the polar bear to survive the cold.

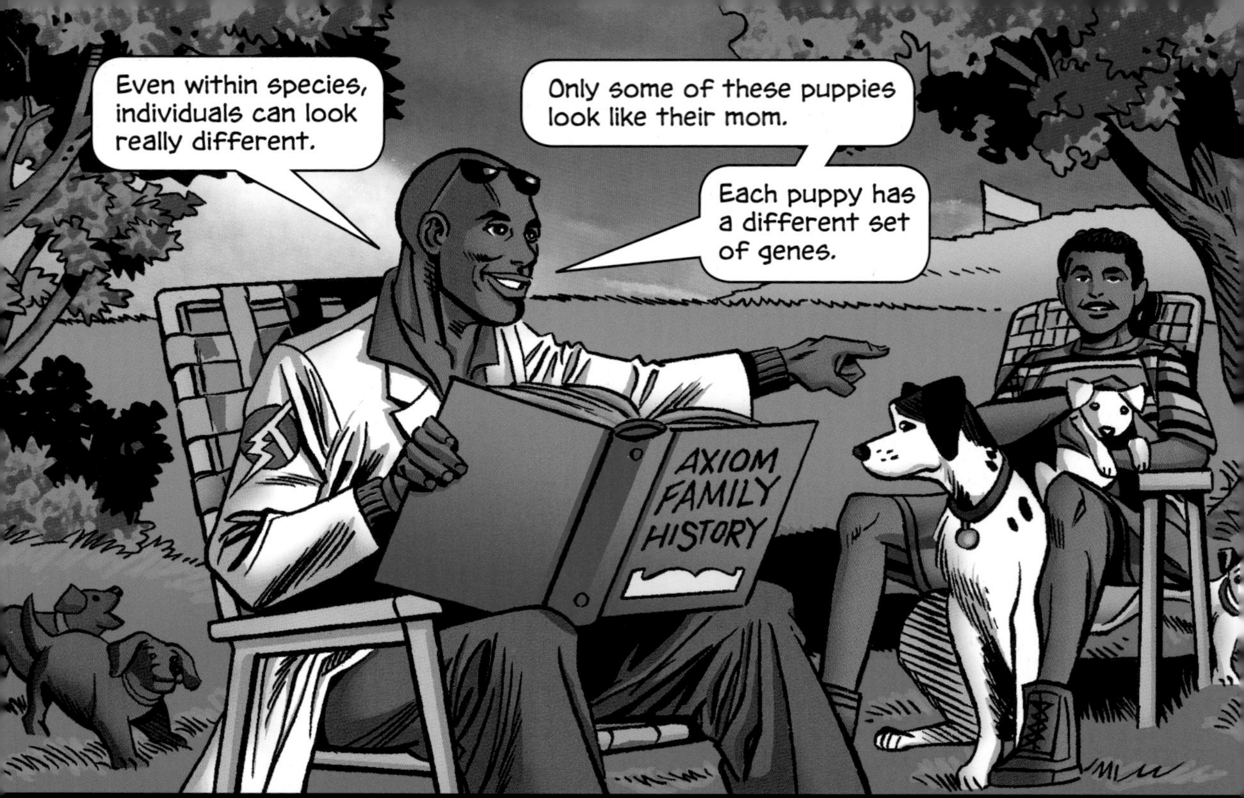
Even within species, individuals can look really different.
Only some of these puppies look like their mom.
Each puppy has a different set of genes.
AXIOM FAMILY HISTORY

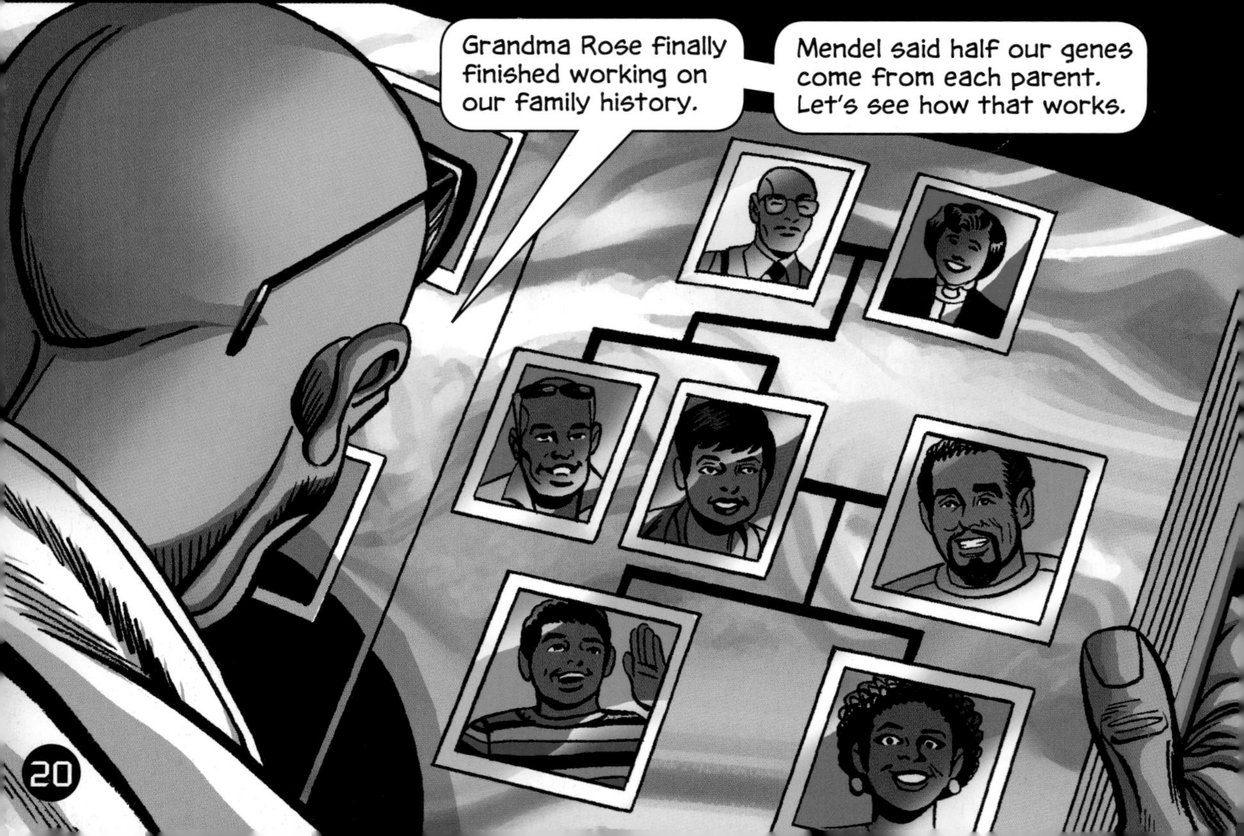
Grandma Rose finally finished working on our family history.
Mendel said half our genes come from each parent. Let's see how that works.

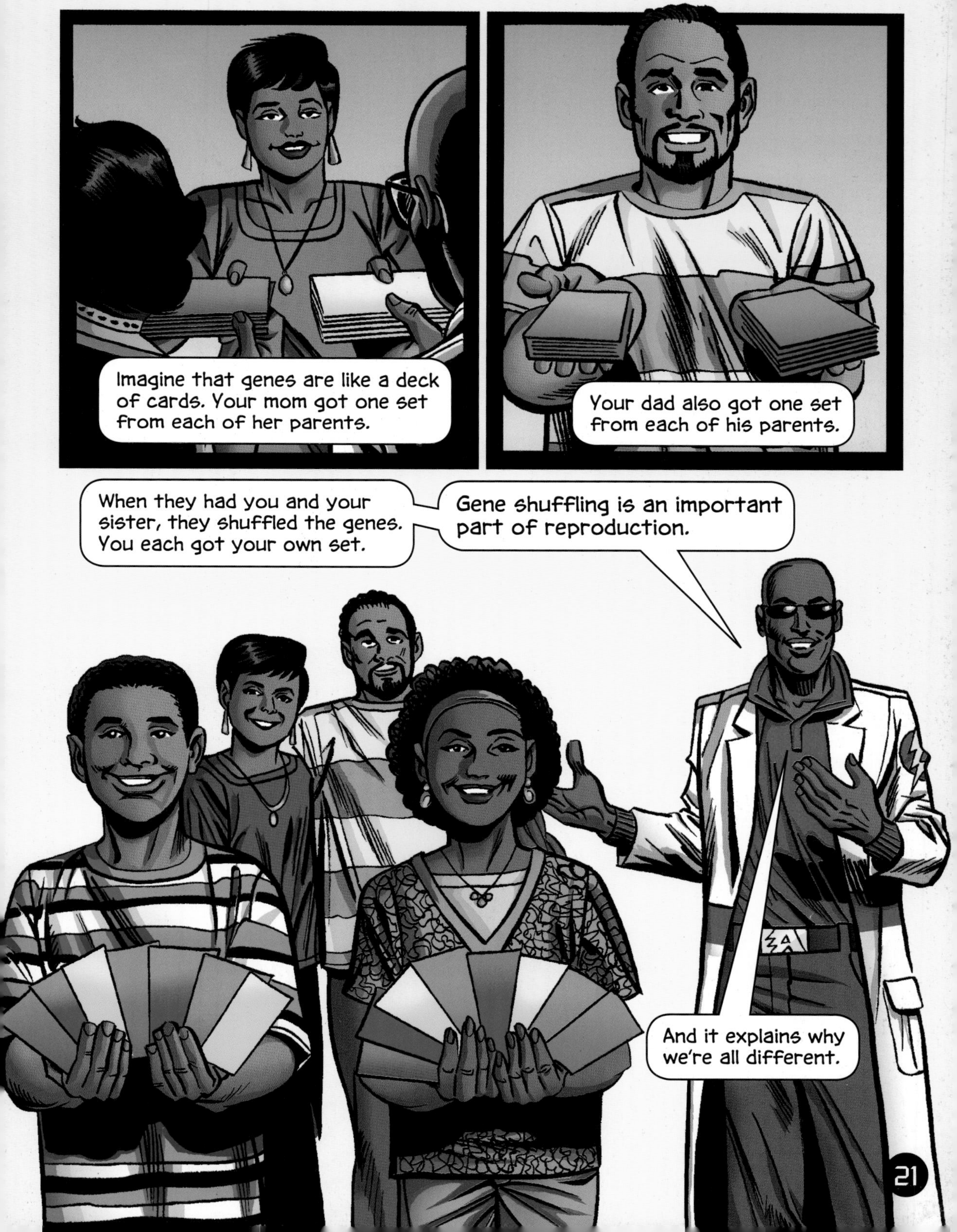

Imagine that genes are like a deck of cards. Your mom got one set from each of her parents.
Your dad also got one set from each of his parents.
When they had you and your sister, they shuffled the genes. You each got your own set.
Gene shuffling is an important part of reproduction.
And it explains why we're all different.

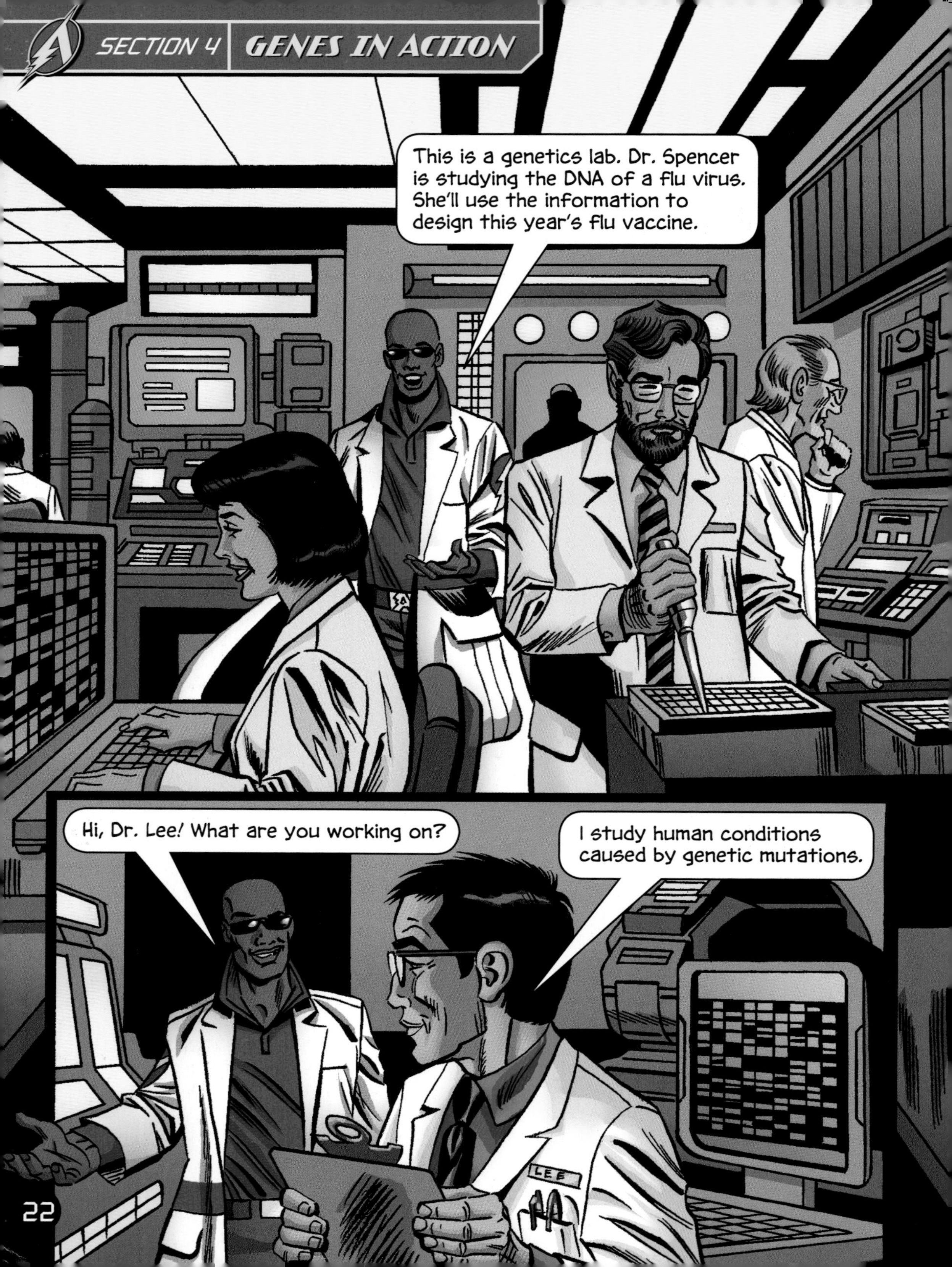
This is a genetics lab. Dr. Spencer is studying the DNA of a flu virus. She'll use the information to design this year's flu vaccine.
Hi, Dr. Lee! What are you working on?
I study human conditions caused by genetic mutations.
LEE

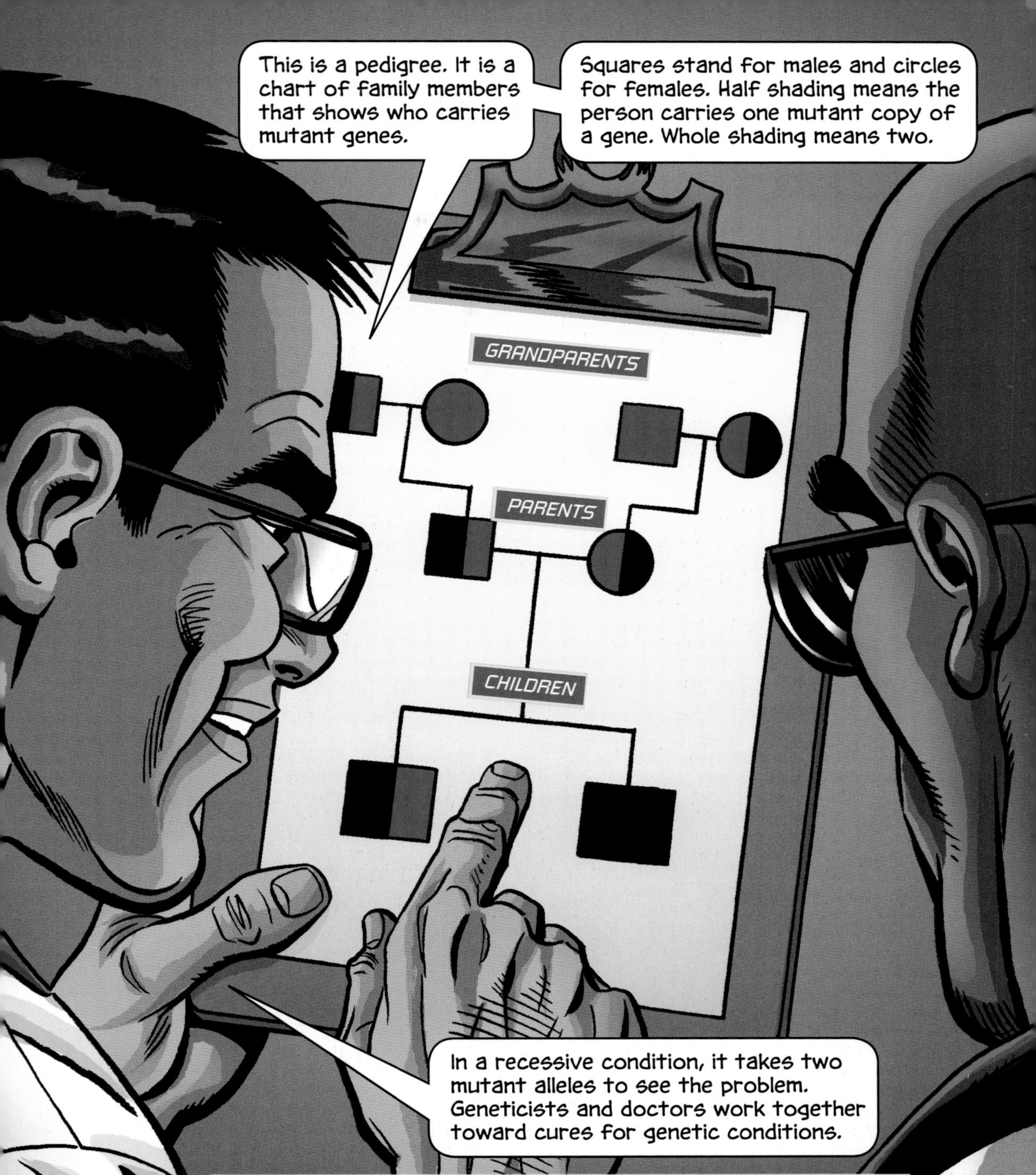

This is a pedigree. It is a chart of family members that shows who carries mutant genes.
Squares stand for males and circles for females. Half shading means the person carries one mutant copy of a gene. Whole shading means two.
GRANDPARENTS
PARENTS
CHILDREN
In a recessive condition, it takes two mutant alleles to see the problem. Geneticists and doctors work together toward cures for genetic conditions.

MUTATIONS

When people discover that they carry mutant genes, they often meet with a genetic counselor. A genetic counselor discusses their chances of having a child with a genetic condition.

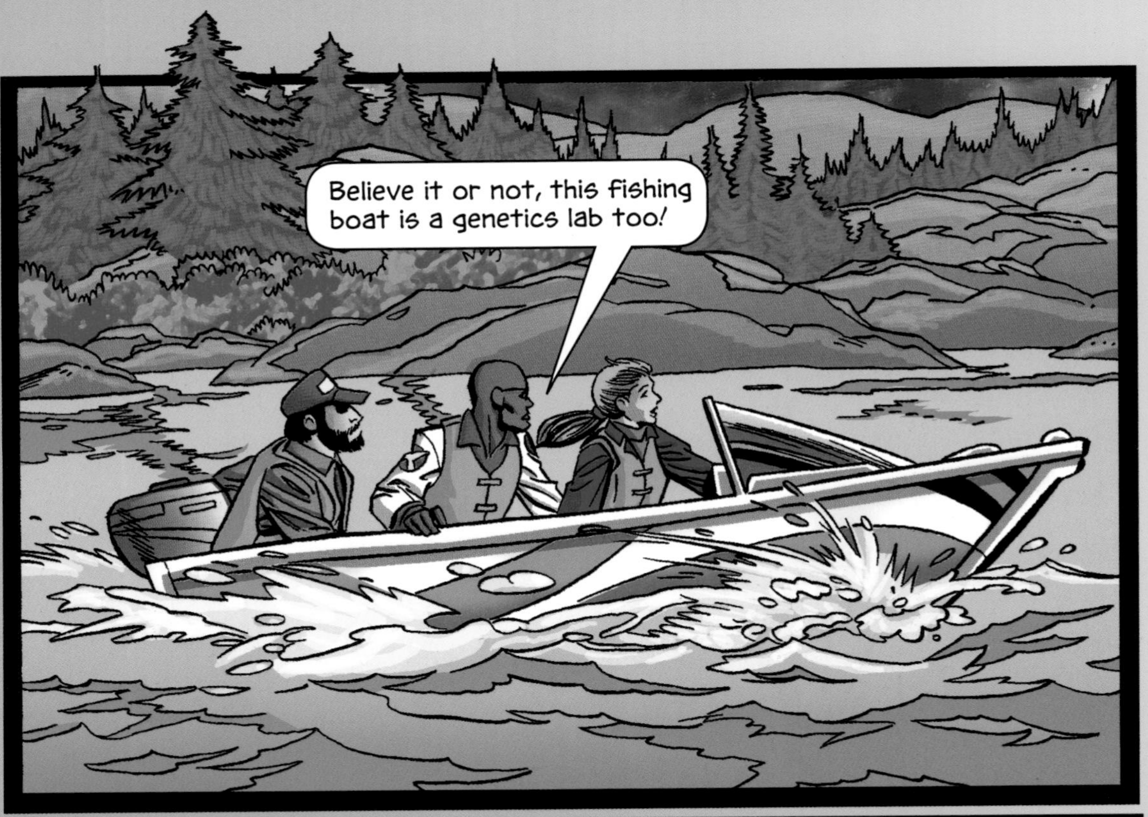
Believe it or not, this fishing boat is a genetics lab too!

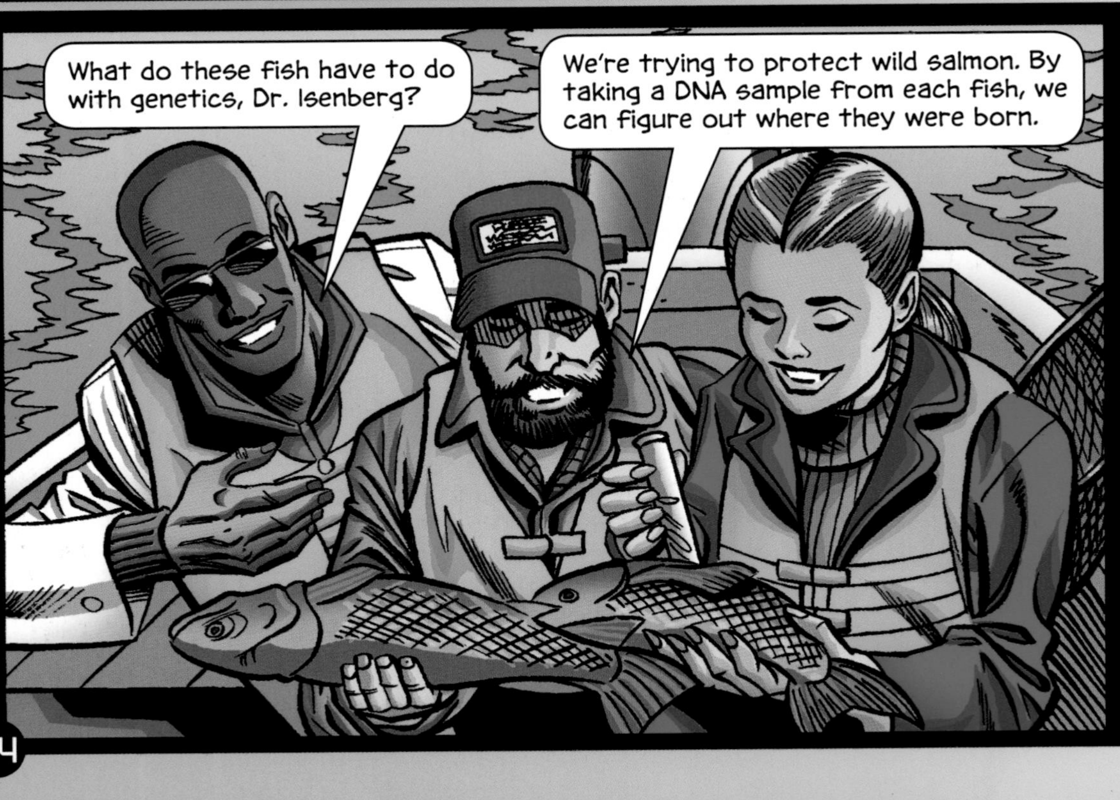
What do these fish have to do with genetics, Dr. Isenberg?
We're trying to protect wild salmon. By taking a DNA sample from each fish, we can figure out where they were born.

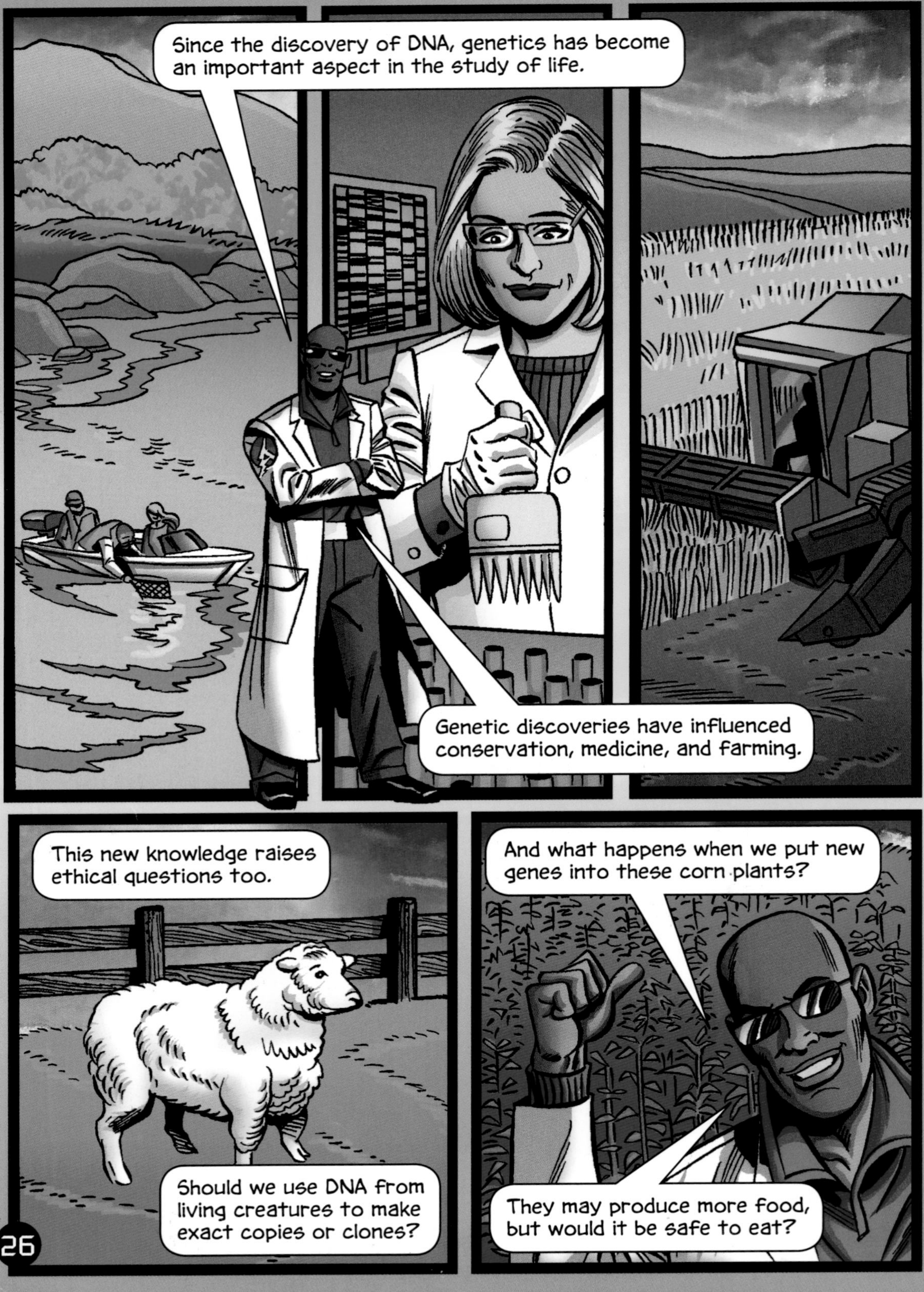
Since the discovery of DNA, genetics has become an important aspect in the study of life.
Genetic discoveries have influenced conservation, medicine, and farming.
This new knowledge raises ethical questions too.
Should we use DNA from living creatures to make exact copies or clones?
And what happens when we put new genes into these corn plants?
They may produce more food, but would it be safe to eat?

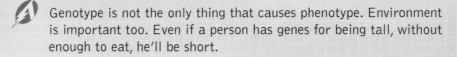
Genotype is not the only thing that causes phenotype. Environment is important too. Even if a person has genes for being tall, without enough to eat, he'll be short.

The condition called Down syndrome occurs when a human child ends up with 47 chromosomes instead of 46.

To make Dolly, the famous sheep clone, scientists took a cell from an adult sheep and removed the DNA. They injected the DNA into an egg cell without any DNA. Then they put the egg inside of a female sheep where it grew into a new lamb. Dolly was an exact genetic copy of the first sheep.

Identical twins are a kind of clone. Very early in development, a fertilized egg splits in half. Each half grows into a baby. They are identical because each twin has exactly the same genes.

Many genes are necessary to tell cells when to divide and when to stop dividing. If a mutation occurs in any of those genes, cells will divide when they aren't supposed to. This results in the disease called cancer.

Genetic modification occurs when a scientist takes a gene from one organism and puts it into another. For example, a gene from bacteria was added to the corn genome. The gene makes a protein that kills caterpillars. The good thing is that farmers don't have to spray corn with insecticide. The bad thing is that the gene could spread to other plants and could even affect human health.

Some geneticists are trying to find cures for common genetic diseases using gene therapy. The idea is to replace damaged or mutated genes with normal ones.

 There are many kinds of genetics. Some geneticists study the genomes of endangered species. Others try to understand how each individual gene gives directions to the body. They may also study phenotypes like height that are caused by many genes working together. Still others use genes to understand how groups of plants and animals have changed over time.

MORE ABOUT

SUPER SCIENTIST

Real name: Maxwell J. Axiom
Hometown: Seattle, Washington
Height: 6' 1"   **Weight:** 192 lbs
Eyes: Brown   **Hair:** None

Super capabilities: Super intelligence; able to shrink to the size of an atom; sunglasses give x-ray vision; lab coat allows for travel through time and space.

Origin: Since birth, Max Axiom seemed destined for greatness. His mother, a marine biologist, taught her son about the mysteries of the sea. His father, a nuclear physicist and volunteer park ranger, schooled Max on the wonders of earth and sky.

One day on a wilderness hike, a megacharged lightning bolt struck Max with blinding fury. When he awoke, Max discovered a newfound energy and set out to learn as much about science as possible. He traveled the globe earning degrees in every aspect of the field. Upon his return, he was ready to share his knowledge and new identity with the world. He had become Max Axiom, Super Scientist.

allele (UH-lee-uhl) — one of two genes in a pair contributed by the parent

base (BAYS) — a building block of DNA; the four bases are adenine, guanine, thymine, and cytosine.

chromosome (KROH-muh-sohm) — a structure inside a cell containing genetic codes that control growth, development, and function of all cells

DNA (dee-en-AY) — the molecule that carries all of the instructions to make a living thing and keeps it working; short for deoxyribonucleic acid.

dominant (DOM-uh-nuhnt) — the gene most likely to produce a trait in offspring

gene (JEEN) — a part of every cell that carries physical and behavioral information passed from parents to their children

genetic mutation (juh-NET-ik myoo-TAY-shun) — a change in an animal's genetic makeup that causes it to develop in a different way

genotype (JEE-noh-tipe) — the genes that produce a phenotype

heredity (huh-RED-uh-tee) — the process by which parents pass traits to their children

nucleus (NOO-klee-uhss) — the part of each cell that contains the genetic material

phenotype (FEE-noh-tipe) — traits you can see, count, or measure

protein (PROH-teen) — a substance found in all living animal and plant cells; protein is necessary for growth and life.

recessive (ruh-SESS-iv) — the gene most likely to stay hidden in offspring

READ MORE

Hartman, Eve, and Wendy Meshbesher. *The Role of Genes*. Sci-Hi: Life Science. Chicago: Raintree, 2009.

Keyser, Amber. *The Basics of Cell Life with Max Axiom, Super Scientist*. Graphic Science. Mankato, Minn.: Capstone Press, 2010

Phelan, Glen. *Double Helix: The Quest to Uncover the Structure of DNA*. Science Quest. Washington, D.C.: National Geographic, 2006.

Simpson, Kathleen. *Genetics: From DNA to Designer Dogs*. National Geographic Investigates Science. Washington, D.C.: National Geographic, 2008.

Stille, Darlene. *Genetics: A Living Blueprint*. Exploring Science. Minneapolis: Compass Point Books, 2006.

INTERNET SITES

FactHound offers a safe, fun way to find Internet sites related to this book. All sites on FactHound have been researched by our staff.

Here's all you do:

Visit *www.facthound.com*

FactHound will fetch the best sites for you!

INDEX

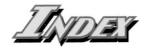